KU-428-686

Artists' Workshop

Landscapes

Penny King & Clare Roundhill

A & C Black · London

Designed by Jane Warring

Illustrations by Lindy Norton

Children's pictures by
Emily Ashworth, Amber Civardi, Camilla Cramsie, Louise Cramsie,
Charlotte Downham, Lara Haworth, Lucinda Howells, Sophie Johns,
Lucy Macdonald Watson, Zoë More O'Ferrall, Gussie Pownall,
Thomas Stofer, Alice Williams, Dusty Williams

Picture research by Sara Elliott

Photographs by Peter Millard

Reprinted 1999, 2002
First paperback edition 1996
First published 1996 in hardback by
A & C Black Publishers Ltd
37 Soho Square, London, W1D 3QZ
www.acblack.com

Created by
Thumbprint Books

Copyright © 1996 Thumbprint Books

ISBN 0-7136-6698-6

Printed and bound in Singapore

A & C Black uses paper produced with elemental chlorine-free pulp,
harvested from managed, sustainable forests.

Cover photograph: Raoul Dufy Open Window at Saint-Jeannet (c. 1926-27)
Dufy was a French artist who painted views of ragattas, racecourses, sea fronts and other landscapes.
He worked quickly, using patches of colour as a background covered with bolder strokes for detail.

Contents

Looking at landscapes

Wherever you live in the world, when you look out of a window you see a view. You might see trees and fields, houses and shops, sky and clouds or shimmering sea. These views are called landscapes.

In this book, there are six landscapes created by artists from different countries. Two of the artists, Monet and Hokusai, painted real places they loved and knew well. They spent a long time looking at the same place in all kinds of weather and at different times of the day, throughout the year.

Klimt and Hundertwasser painted imaginary landscapes to show how they would like the world to be. They often used particularly glowing colours and patterns.

O'Keeffe and Burchfield had strong feelings about the places they painted. They did not paint places exactly as they were, but tried to show their special atmosphere by using unusual colours and shapes.

Landscape artists want the people who look at their pictures to feel as if they could walk into them and wander around. Sometimes they include an empty chair in their paintings so that the viewer can imagine sitting down and becoming part of the picture.

Painting a landscape is a good way of reminding yourself of a place you have visited. Spend time looking closely at the colours, shapes and details. Decide how the place makes you feel. Does it make you feel calm or energetic, happy or sad?

One way to make a picture look like a real place is to use perspective. This means you have to paint the things closest to you bigger than those in the distance.

Notice where the land or sea appears to meet the sky. This is called the horizon.

If you prefer, paint landscapes from your imagination or from dreams, like the picture above of the upside-down houses. Think what an overgrown garden, an alien planet or a hidden city might look like.

Make your picture as fantastic as you can. Exaggerate the shapes and use vivid colours.

Views of a volcano

Mount Fuji is the highest peak in Japan and one of its most sacred places. People went on long and difficult journeys to visit and worship this mountain.
A famous Japanese artist, called Hokusai, who lived over 200 years ago, made many wonderful woodcut prints of it.

Katsushika Hokusai Fuji in Clear Weather 1823-29, British Museum, London.

Hokusai created over 30,000 designs in his life, but he is probably best-known for his set of 36 prints of Mount Fuji. He made these when he was nearly 70 years old. The prints show Mount Fuji from all sides and in all kinds of weather.

Hokusai used bold colours and strong shapes in his prints. In this one, the solid red of the mountain helps it to stand out well against the patterns of clouds and trees. In his famous picture, *The Wave*, Mount Fuji can be seen behind a stormy sea.

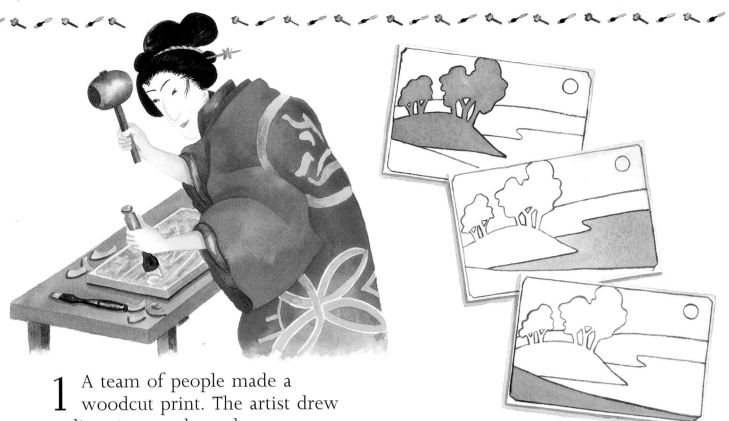

1 A team of people made a woodcut print. The artist drew outlines on see-through paper. A block cutter pasted the sketch face down on to a block of wood. Using a knife, he cut everything away except the outline.

3 A separate block was needed for every colour in the picture. Using an outline print, the artist drew in the design for each colour. The block cutter cut away everything that was not this colour.

2 This block was called the key block. A printer covered it with ink and put a piece of paper on top. He smoothed the paper to make sure that the whole picture was printed. He made lots of these outline prints.

4 The printer pressed a piece of paper on to each coloured block in turn. Each time, he lined the paper up with the raised corner of the block, so that all the parts of the picture were in the right place.

Mighty mountains

It would take you a very long time to do a woodcut like Hokusai's. However, there are several easy ways of making pictures that will look like woodcuts. Before you start any printing, it's a good idea to plan your picture by drawing it on a sheet of paper first.

Plasticine prints

Roll some Plasticine flat, about 3 mm thick. Cut it into a square with a knife. Using the point of a pencil or a knitting needle, scratch a volcano in it, with steam whooshing out of the top.

Cover the volcano, steam and background with different coloured poster paints. Press a piece of paper, larger than your picture, on to the Plasticine. Carefully peel it off. You now have a print of your picture.

Art tile prints

Scratch a picture of a mountain in the middle of an art tile. Cover the slopes with trees and some houses. Put stars and a moon in the sky. Coat the tile with printing ink and press a piece of paper on to it. Peel the paper off. To make a frieze, let the ink dry before recoating the tile with another colour.

Mount Fuji erupts

Imagine you are in Japan about 300 years ago, when Mount Fuji last erupted. Paint a picture of what you think this must have looked like. Use reds, oranges and yellows for the flames and dark grey for the lava and smoke.

Golden garden

This glowing, golden tree with its twisting, curling branches is a sketch for part of a huge frieze designed by Gustav Klimt, a famous Austrian artist. The finished picture was created in a long mosaic of marble inlaid with gold, enamel and semi-precious stones.

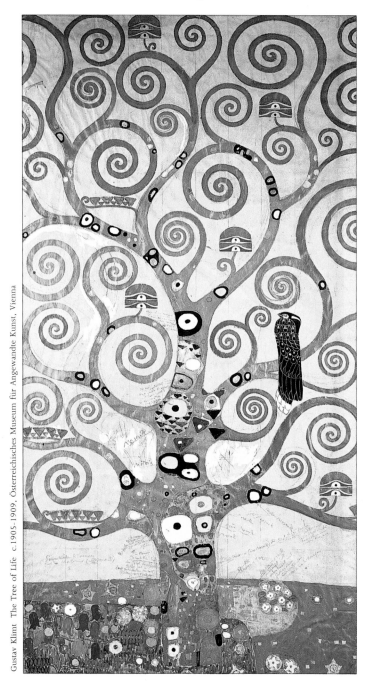

Gustav Klimt   The Tree of Life   c.1905-1909, Österreichisches Museum für Angewandte Kunst, Vienna

Klimt wanted the frieze to seem magical and fantastic, rather than realistic. He made a very careful and detailed sketch for the mosaic maker to follow. Klimt used paints, crayons and coloured shapes, as well as real gold and silver leaf in his design.

The mosaic was made to decorate the dining room of Adolphe Stoclet, a very rich man who lived in Brussels. The two huge panels which face one another each have a tree as a main image. One is the Tree of Knowledge and the other is the Tree of Life.

Under one of the two big trees there is a dancing girl and under the other is a man and a woman hugging. Klimt wanted to show a perfect world where people were always happy.

These people have normal-looking heads and hands, but their clothes are covered with jewel-like patterns. Klimt was more interested in decoration than in trying to make people and objects look real and rounded.

When he was older, Klimt did not like to talk much and preferred to spend his time alone. One of the most important things in his life was his garden which gave him many ideas for paintings. This is a picture of his garden in bloom. His flowers fill every bit of space on the canvas.

Trees and flowers

Design your own magical Tree of Life with golden branches covered in delicious fruit. Or paint a picture of a happy person dancing in a fantastic garden. You could also create a garden full of wild and wonderful flowers reaching up to the sun.

The Tree of Life

Draw a tree with curling, twisting branches on a big piece of gold paper. Cut it out and glue it on to a bright coloured background. Make a mosaic path with small squares and triangles cut from different coloured shiny paper.

Cut out curvy tin foil leaves, juicy felt fruits and colourful wiggly paper cut-outs to decorate your tree. You might like to add some pretty birds perching in the branches.

A merry dancer

In the middle of a sheet of paper, draw a happy picture of a dancer, wearing loose clothes and leaping with delight.

Make the head, hands and feet look as realistic as possible, but decorate the clothes with fantastic patterns to give them a fairytale look. Like Klimt, you can use anything you want - crayons, paint, shiny mosaic pieces, gold and silver paper.

Draw, paint, or use paper cut-outs to decorate the background with flowers, bushes and long, tickly grass.

Mosaic flower bed

Practise drawing flowers on scrap paper. Give some big, fat petals, others long pointy petals and some tiny petals.

Then draw flowers like these on brightly coloured gummed paper. Cut them out and stick them on to a coloured background. Add gummed-paper leaves and wiggly stems. Try to fill the whole page with flowers, leaves and tangled stems.

The waterlily pond

This picture was painted by Claude Monet, a French artist. When he was an old man, Monet spent a lot of time painting pictures of the lily pond with its Japanese bridge in his garden at Giverny, in France. This is just one of 18 views of the bridge that he painted in 1899.

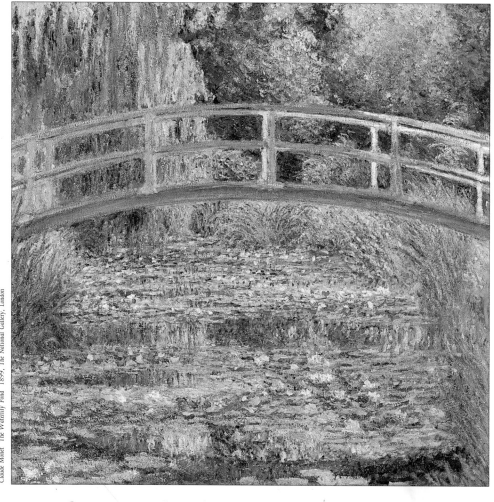

Claude Monet The Waterlily Pond 1899, The National Gallery, London

Monet was one of a group of artists called the Impressionists. They painted everyday scenes, often out of doors. Impressionists did not paint what they saw in detail. They were more interested in catching the effects of light on a scene.

Monet painted this same view of the lilypond at all sorts of different times - in sunny and cloudy weather and in the morning and the evening. He wanted to show how the look and mood of a place changed in different light.

Monet painted quickly. When art critics first saw his pictures, they thought they looked unfinished.

He used dots and dashes of colour to give the impression of flowers, leaves and rippling water, and painted longer wider strokes for bigger areas, such as buildings.

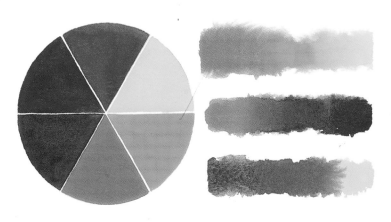

Monet never used black in his pictures. For shadows, he either mixed dark colours or used complementary ones.

Look at this colour wheel. Red, blue and yellow, the pure colours, are called primary colours. The complementary colours are orange, green and purple. Each one is a mixture of the two primary colours on either side of it. Try mixing them for yourself.

Woods and water

Paint some pictures of outdoor places that you know and particularly enjoy, such as a garden, woods or a lake. You don't need to put in every detail of exactly what they look like. Instead, create a colourful scene, which shows other people what these places feel like.

Shimmering water

When Monet painted water, he used streaks of colour to show ripples. He used white and different shades of yellow to show the glint and sparkle of sunshine on the water's surface. He used dark greens and blues for the reflections of trees and bushes. With poster paints and a fat paintbrush, use Monet's techniques to create your own picture of shimmering water. Add pretty waterlilies or some shadowy reflections of trees.

Autumn colours

Paint a glowing autumn picture of a tree or a whole forest, with leaves in all sorts of shades of orange, yellow, red and brown. Don't bother to paint every leaf. Do as the Impressionists did. Paint a knobbly tree trunk with branches, and then dab on overlapping splodges of autumn colours for the leaves.

A flowery garden

Mix as many different shades of green as you can. Use them to paint a picture of a leafy garden. Blend the colours into one another, brushing in different directions to make your picture look alive. Use dark colours for shadows and light colours for the brighter places. Dot bright pink, red, blue, orange and yellow flowers all over your garden.

Spectacular sunrise

Have you ever been awake early enough to see the sun rising? This picture, by an American artist, called Georgia O'Keeffe, is her idea of a spectacular sunrise in Texas. She loved to be out early in the wide open spaces of America with the sky towering above her.

Georgia O'Keeffe Sunrise with Little Clouds No II 1916, Private Collection

O'Keeffe has used only the primary colours (red, blue and yellow), which she has mixed together to create the glowing colours of the sky. There are three parts to the picture - the top shows the night sky and the bottom, the dark ground. The rising sun in the middle of the painting brightens up the whole scene.

In her painting, O'Keeffe has shown the sky and clouds but she has used unusual colours and shapes taken from her imagination. Although some people might think that this picture just looks like a sandwich of colour, others can easily spot the sun rising at the beginning of a new day.

Georgia O'Keeffe grew up in the countryside, but later she went to live in New York. Here she lived in a flat on the 28th floor of the very first skyscraper to be built. She was so excited about these modern tall buildings that she painted over 20 pictures of them, often showing them at night. This famous painting of hers is called the American Radiator Building.

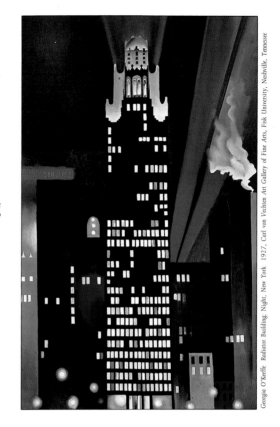

Georgia O'Keeffe Radiator Building: Night, New York 1927, Carl von Vechten Art Gallery of Fine Arts, Fisk University, Nashville, Tennessee

The artist is best known for her pictures of flowers. She painted them very close up so that every detail and shade of colour could be seen. It seems almost as if she was looking through a magnifying glass as she painted.

Every year, O'Keeffe went to her house in New Mexico. While she was there, she started to paint pictures of the bones of animals that had died in the desert. She particularly liked the contrasting look of the stark white bones against the bright blue sky. Her husband and friends often found themselves sharing the car with piles of bones that she had collected.

Sensational skies

Georgia O'Keeffe did not believe in simply copying the landscapes that she saw. She liked to use her imagination and her feelings to help make her paintings unusual and exciting. Try painting your own sunset pictures, but make them more dream like than realistic.

Rolling clouds

Look up at the sky when the sun is just setting. Use pastels or chalk to sketch the clouds that you can see. Start by making the clouds white. To make grey clouds, add a little black. Add red to show the sunset.

Blend the colours with your finger or a small piece of cotton wool. Don't worry if the clouds look unreal - the more magical they look, the better.

Spectacular sunrise

You only need to use the three primary colours - red, blue and yellow - to make this spectacular sunrise. Using a fat brush, wet a piece of paper all over with water. Imagine that your piece of paper is divided into three parts.

Paint purply blues for the sky and reds and oranges for the clouds over the top third of your paper. In the middle, use lighter oranges and yellows to show that the day is just beginning. On the bottom, paint a rich earth colour, rippling sea or rolling hills.

Remember that you are painting an imaginary picture. Work quickly and don't worry about making it look exactly like real life.

Far horizons

The horizon is the place where the sky seems to touch the land. To create your own horizon painting, first fold a piece of paper in half.

Over the top half, paint a dark, sky with big, black clouds and bolts of lightning zig-zagging down to the ground. Paint fields over the bottom half.

When your painting is dry, add some trees. Any tree that you put on the horizon should be smaller than the trees in the foreground.

A frosty forest

This forest, shown on a freezing cold night, was painted with watercolours by an American artist called Charles Burchfield. Although he has used only a few colours, the artist has managed to catch the wintry feeling.

Charles E. Burchfield Orion in December 1959, National Museum of American Art, Washington D.C.

Earth and sky seem to meet in Burchfield's picture. You can see that some of the stars have slipped down among the trees. The trees are outlined in black which give them a slightly ghostly feeling

The stars in the sky are reflected by twinkling snowflakes on the frosty ground. Burchfield has made them shimmer and sparkle by giving each of them a contrasting black outline and a halo of white paint.

When Burchfield was a young boy, he liked to go for long walks in the forest. He noticed the patterns and light all around him. Sometimes, to help him to concentrate, he lay on the ground with his eyes shut tight.

Burchfield enjoyed the sound of the wind whistling through the trees, the smell of the forest and the feel of the ground beneath him. When he became an artist, he drew on the powerful memories of his visits to the woods to paint many of his pictures.

In his painting, Burchfield has shown a constellation of stars, called Orion. In Greek mythology, Orion was a hunter. He was accidentally killed by a goddess, called Artemis. Artemis was so sorry about what she had done that she turned Orion into a constellation of stars so that he would always be remembered.

If you look carefully, you can see that the three stars in a row show Orion's belt, and the two big stars are his huge shoulders.

Winter wonders

Imagine that it's late at night and everything is still and silent. Delicate snowflakes are falling on the dark, leafless trees and the stars are glimmering in the sky. Paint a picture of how you think this would look, using the same wintry colours as Burchfield.

Moonlit scene

Use white, black, blue and brown to paint a landscape scene in the middle of a dark night. Add a starry sky and a shining moon. Make the stars shimmer by giving them constrasting outlines. Think about the pale night-time colours and the silence all around to give your picture a mysterious feeling.

Stars and snowflakes

To create these incredible snowflakes and stunning stars you'll need a water-based black felt-tip pen and some absorbent kitchen paper or blotting paper.

Cut the paper into circles or squares. Draw star or snowflake shapes on the paper with the felt-tip pen and then drip water on to your picture. As the water spreads over the surface, it will make the black ink split into a rainbow of colours.

Scraperboard snowscene

For this technique, you'll need a scraperboard and scraper tool which you can buy in an art shop.

Make a sketch of the scene you are going to create. Draw the outline of a forest full of bare trees. Add flurries of snowflakes and some twinkling stars. Complete your picture with stiff, frosty grass.

Use the scraping tool to scratch your winter landscape on the scraperboard. Don't worry if you make a mistake, as it is very easy to turn the mark into something else.

Happy houses

How would you like to live in one of these brilliantly coloured, crazy looking houses? The artist who created them is an Austrian, called Friedrich Hundertwasser. He feels that if people live in bright and cheerful homes, they have happier and more interesting lives.

Hundertwasser 637a Waiting Houses 1969 © 1996 Joram Harel, Vienna, Austria

To Hundertwasser, colour is the most important thing. He feels that heaven must be a colourful, bright place, while hell must be dull and grey. He always frames his pictures in black because he thinks it makes the colours shine like jewels.

The artist often signs his pictures with different names. He has signed this picture of a row of domed houses, 'Regentag', which means 'rainy day'. He chose this name because he loves to look at bright colours sparkling through the rain.

Hundertwasser has designed and built many houses. This is a famous one he built in Vienna, called 'Hundertwasserhaus'.

He wanted to build homes for ordinary people which were as fantastic and dreamlike as the incredible palaces built for rich rulers. Each flat is completely different and none of the windows and doors is the same. Hundertwasser planted trees on top of the building to give both shade and colour, as well as to clean the air.

This unusual artist often adds colourful onion-shaped domes to the houses he designs or paints.

They look just like the domes on this beautiful building in Moscow, called Saint Basil's Cathedral. He thinks the onion shape means richness and happiness.

Dreamlike dwellings

Imagine that you have been asked to design some houses. You can use really bright colours and put the doors and windows wherever you like. The roofs can have plants growing on them, or they could be shaped like vegetables or fruit.

Swirly houses

Use some bright jewel-like colours to paint a row of houses. Mix the three primary colours - red, yellow and blue - as well as black and white. Look at the colour wheel on page 15 for tips on mixing.

Add some PVA glue and flour to the paint to make it thick and shiny. Cut out a small rectangle of stiff card. Snip zig-zags in one end. This is a paint comb.

Paint one house at a time on separate pieces of paper. Before the paint dries, scrape swirly patterns in it with your paint comb. Cut out the houses and glue them on stiff black paper. Add shiny windows.

Twinkly palace

Collect fake fur, sequins, scraps of bright fabric and felt to make this shining palace. Coloured pipecleaners are perfect for the swirls. Use a piece of shiny paper for the background.

Decorate your palace with fur-fabric. Add odd-shaped towers cut out of bright fabric or shiny paper. Decorate them with sequins, pipe-cleaners and glitter. Glue a sun or a moon and some shiny paper stars all over the background.

Soaring skyscraper

Hundertwasser often paints buildings with lots of windows in all sorts of shapes and sizes. Look around you and see how many different shaped windows you can spot.

Use a dark felt-tip pen to draw the outline of a skyscraper. Cut out and glue on silver foil windows. Outline the windows with another dark colour. Use brightly coloured felt-tip pens to decorate your tall building.

More about the artists

Katsushika Hokusai

(1760 - 1849   Japanese)
Fuji in Clear Weather 1823-29

Hokusai became an artist's assistant at the age of 15 and worked as an artist for more than 70 years. Some of his best work was done when he was a very old man, aged over 80. He is best known for his landscapes, but he also illustrated books, designed greetings cards and drew many portraits. He enjoyed painting huge mythological figures at festivals, watched by crowds of spectators.

Gustav Klimt

(1826 - 1918   Austrian)
The Tree of Life c.1905-1909

Gustav Klimt came from a family of artists. He and his brother ran a business painting pictures on the interiors of people's houses and grand buildings, such as the theatre, museum and University of Vienna. He later became famous for painting portraits of rich society women. Klimt also designed fabrics, dresses and jewellery.

Claude Monet

(1840 - 1926   French)
The Waterlily Pond 1899

Monet often painted out of doors, showing views of the countryside, the seaside or boats on the river. He also painted pictures of railway stations, cathedrals and buildings in cities. He often did a series of pictures of the same view, such as haystacks or poplar trees. He wanted to show how the look of these views changed in different light. During the last forty years of his life, he created a magnificent garden at Giverny, in France, and painted many pictures of its exotic flowers.

Georgia O'Keeffe

(1887 - 1986   American)
Sunrise with Little Clouds No II 1916

Georgia O'Keeffe decided that she wanted to become an artist when she was still a child. The scenery and objects that she saw on her many travels inspired most of her pictures. O'Keeffe liked to paint outside and she is best known for her detailed pictures of flowers, shells, rocks and pieces of wood. She also painted incredible bird's eye views of rivers, roads and rolling clouds. She kept in her memory the way they looked when she saw them out of aeroplane windows.

Charles Burchfield

(1893 - 1967   American)
Orion in December 1959

Burchfield's early paintings are scenes of Ohio, in America, the place where he grew up. He believed that looking hard at landscapes would help him understand God. He liked to concentrate on the sounds, smells and sights of nature and tried to show its power in his paintings. For a time, he worked as a designer in a wallpaper factory, which made him particularly interested in patterns.

Friedrich Hundertwasser

(Born 1928   Austrian)
Waiting Houses 1969

Hundertwasser's work is inspired by nature. He hopes that his pictures might help make the world a more peaceful place. He puts trees and grass on top of the buildings he creates and never uses straight lines in his paintings, because they don't exist in nature. He recycles materials, often painting on used envelopes and making his own clothes and shoes from scraps of fabric.

Other things to do

1 Make a textured landscape print. Sketch a picture on a large sheet of paper. Find objects with textures, such as leaves, a sponge, string, cotton wool and corrugated paper. Press them one at a time into poster paint and then on to scrap paper. See what patterns they make. Print the patterns you like best on to your landscape picture.

3 Draw or paint your favourite view on some stiff card. Make a window frame for it by gluing long strips of paper on to it. Add curtains made of fabric or tissue paper. Hang the picture on your bedroom wall to look like an extra window.

2 Build a fantastic model landscape of an alien planet. Is your planet hot or cold, dry or wet? Do the plants have big leaves or none at all? What colours are they? Imagine the shape, size and materials of the buildings. Use scrunched-up paper, foil, yogurt pots and other odds and ends.

4 Paint a mural for your bedroom wall on a roll of lining paper or on the back of some spare wallpaper. Imagine you are standing on top of a mountain and that you can see views all around you. There may be hills, rivers, forests, mountains, towns or big cities.

Index

Acknowledgements
The publishers are grateful to the following institutes and individuals for permission to reproduce the illustrations on the pages mentioned.
Tate Gallery, London/© DACS 1996: cover; The British Museum, London: 6; Österreichisches Museum für Angewandte Kunst, Vienna: 10; Reproduced by courtesy of the Trustees, The National Gallery, London: 14; Private collection © The Georgia O'Keeffe Foundation, Abiquiu, New Mexico / © ARS, NY and DACS, London 1996 / Photo by Malcolm Varon, NYC/© 1995: 18; Collection of Fisk University, Nashville, Tennessee / © ARS, NY and DACS, London 1996: 19; National Museum of American Art, Washington DC / Art Resource, NY: 22; © 1995/1996 Joram Harel, Vienna, Austria: 26.